Flowers and Butterflies HAND DRAWN Coloring Book

Left Handed Version

Kay D Johnson

Copyright © 2018 by Kay D. Johnson

All rights reserved.
No part of this book may be reproduced or transmitted in any form or electronic or mechanical means, including photocopying, recording, or by any information storage and retrieval system, without the written permission of the publisher, except where permitted by law.

Johnson, Kay D
Flowers and Butterflies Hand Drawn Coloring Book Left Handed Version

ISBN 978-1-989194-93-5 (pkb)

Enjoying this Coloring Book?
Please leave a review!
I would love to hear your feedback.
Thank you for purchasing my product.
Your support is greatly appreciated.

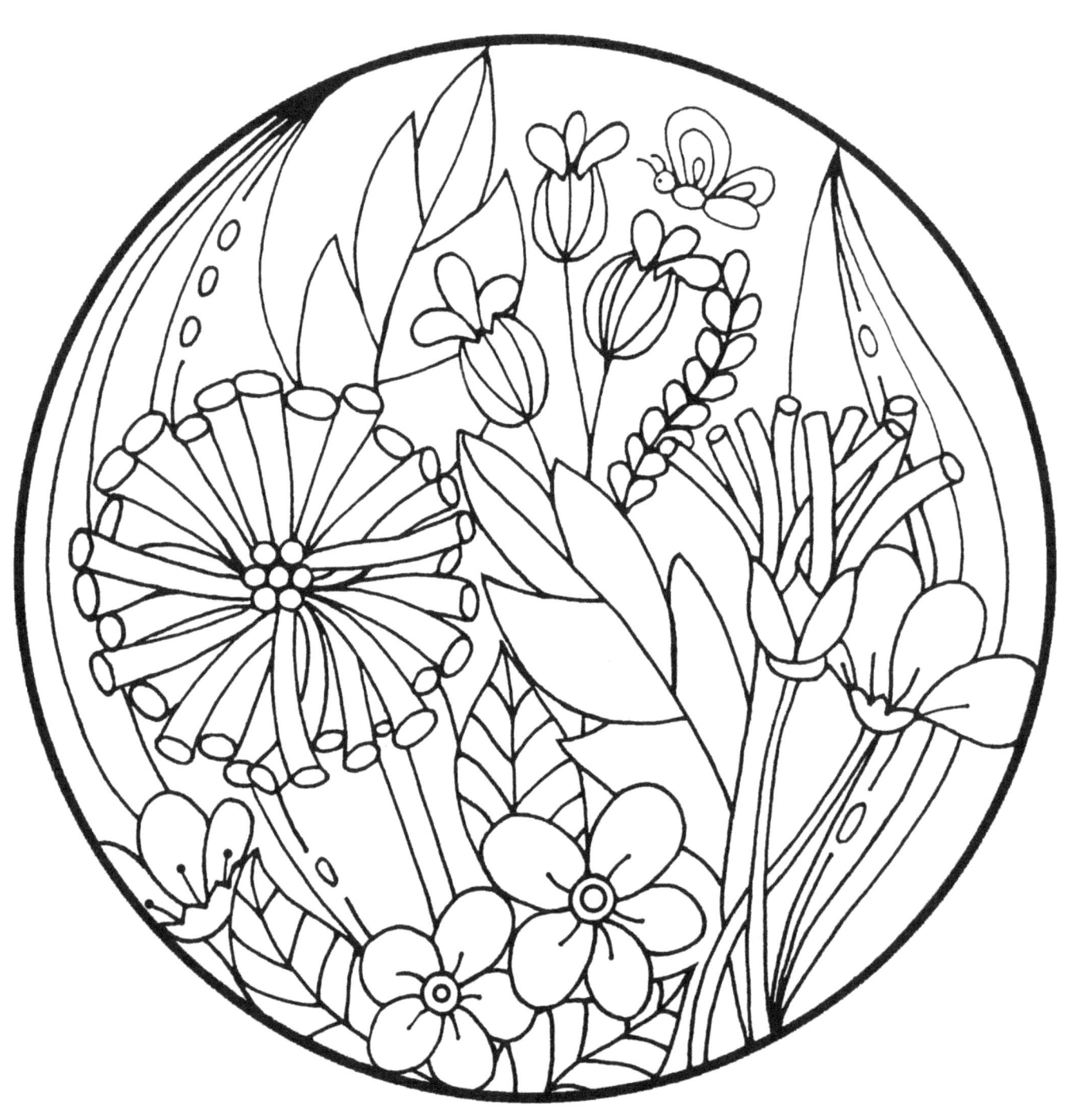

...

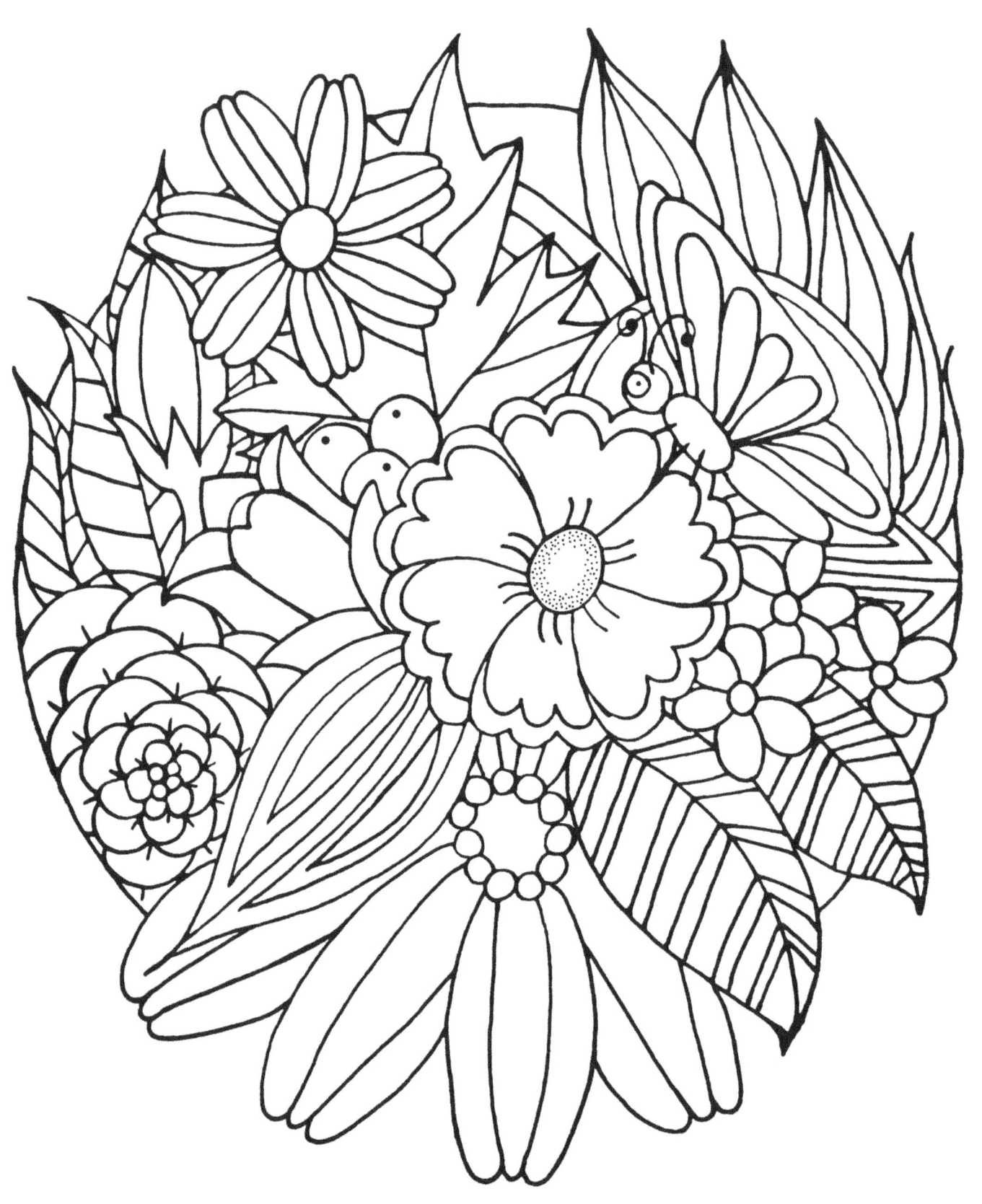

...

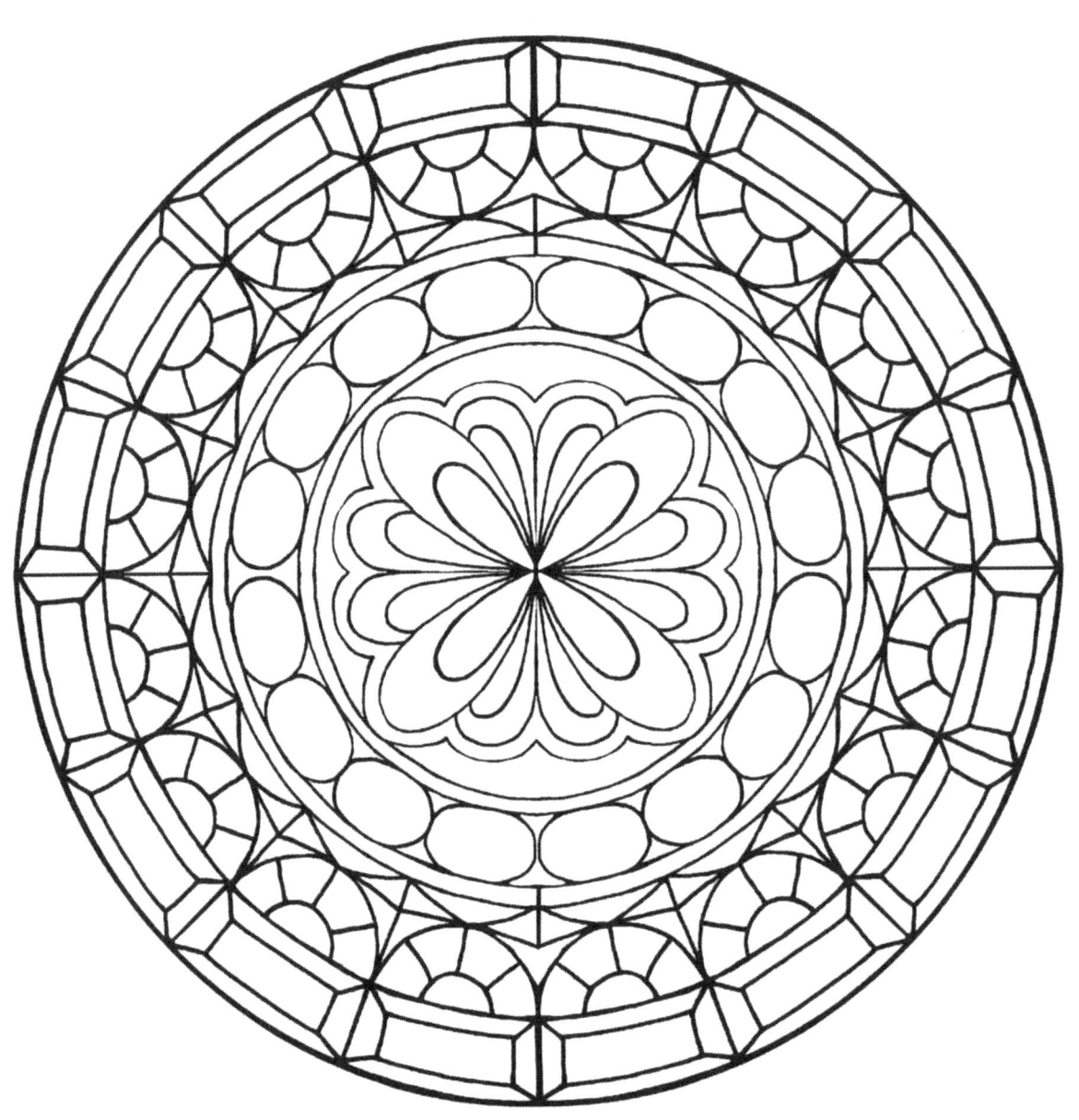

...

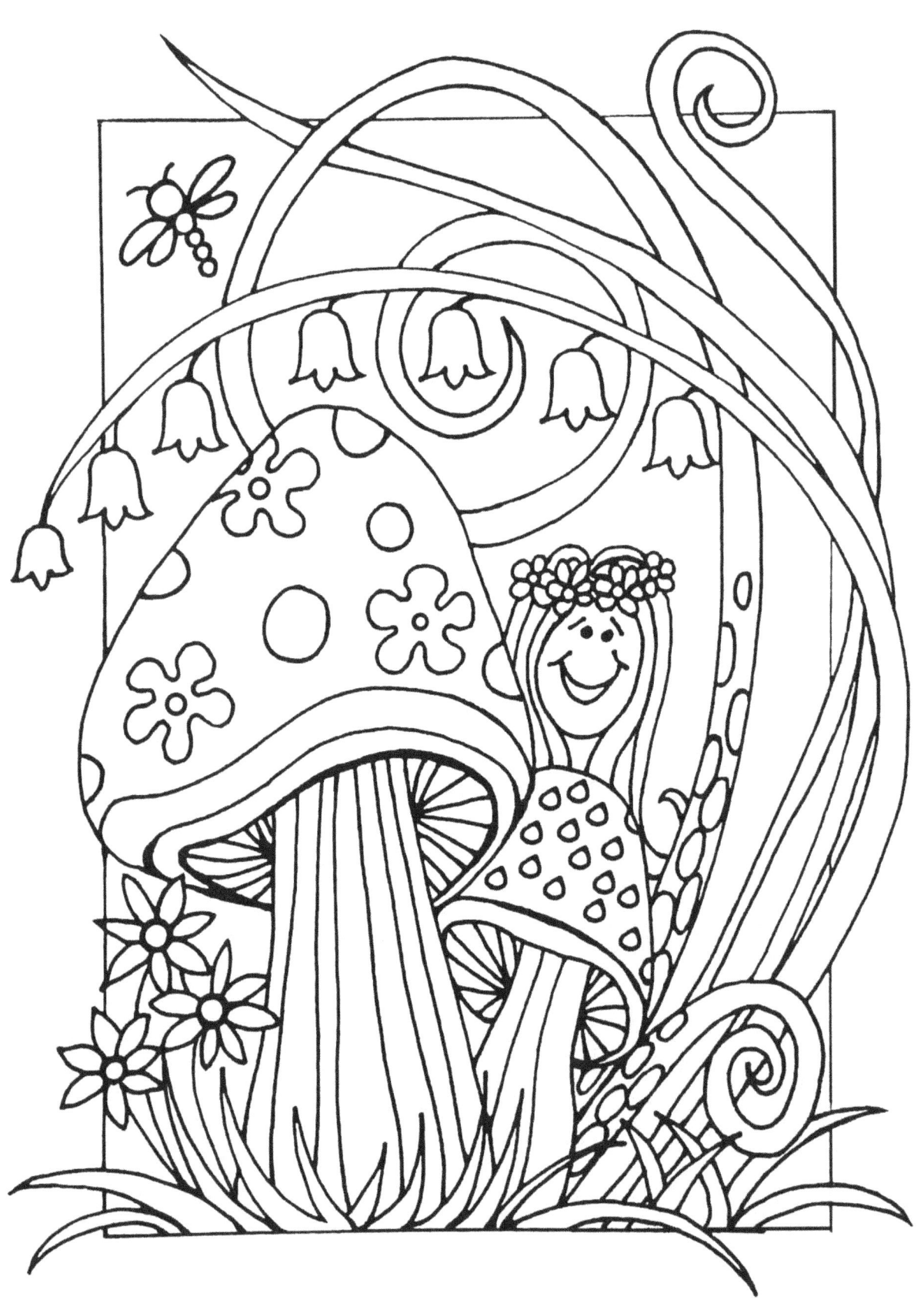

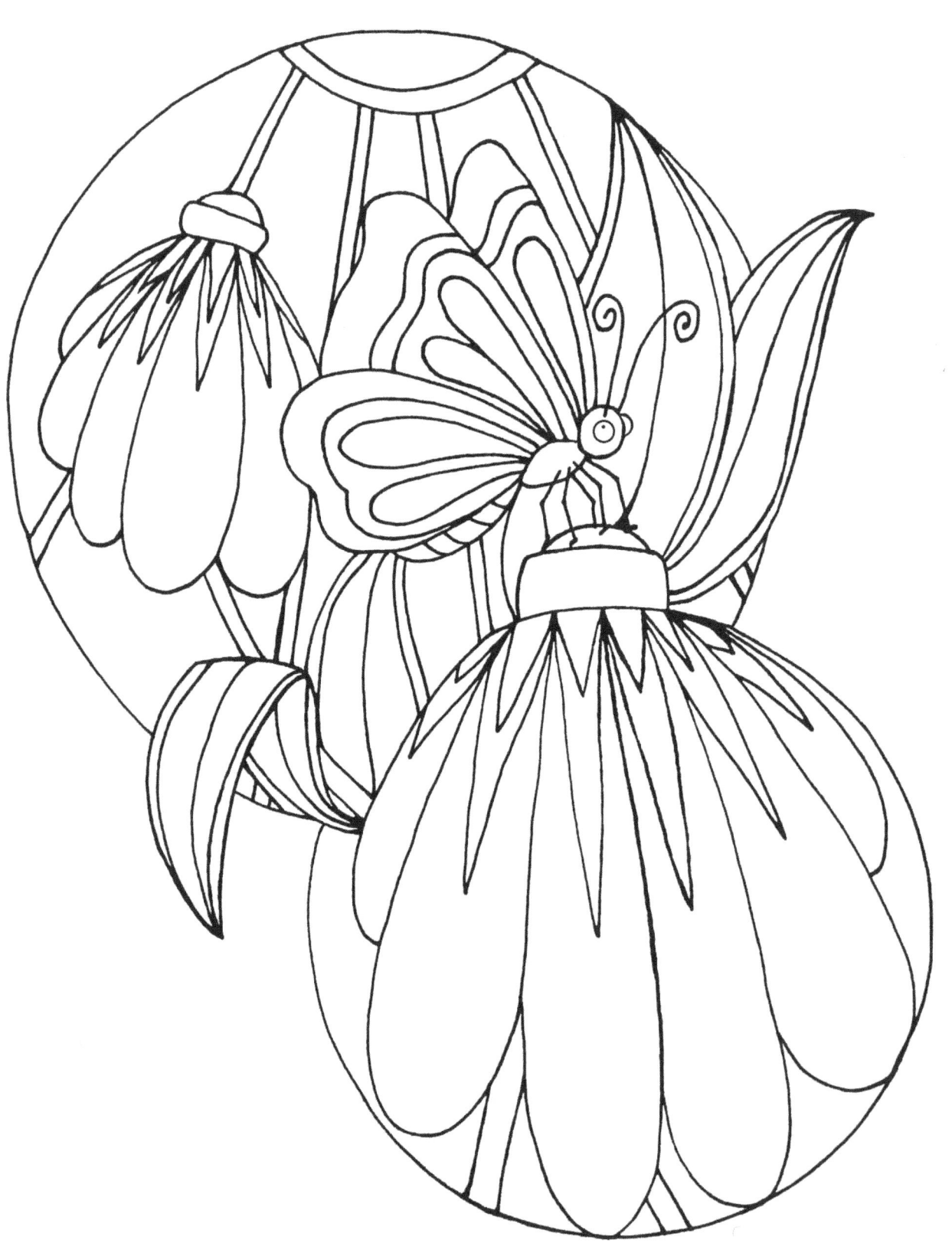

...

…

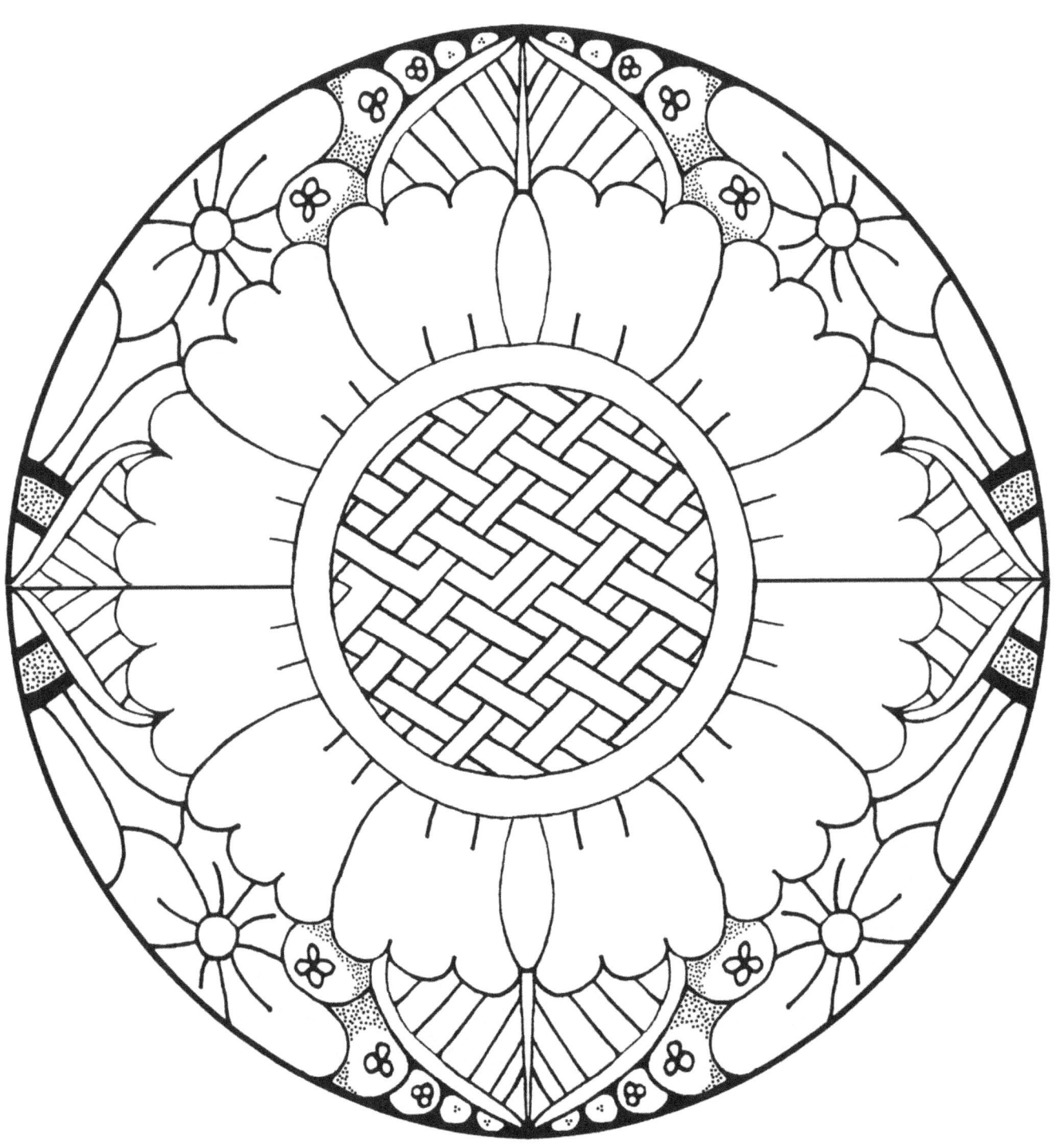

...

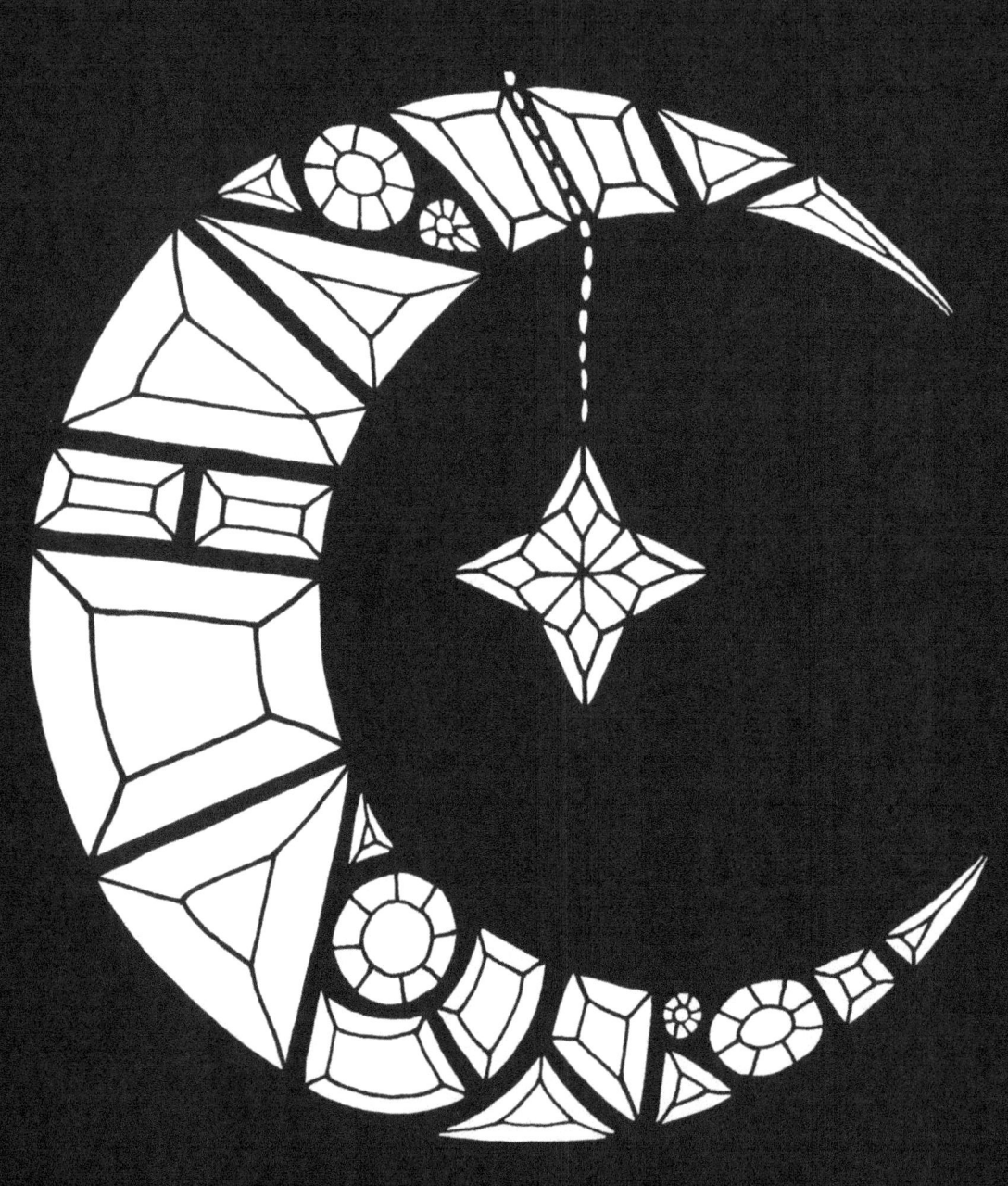

...

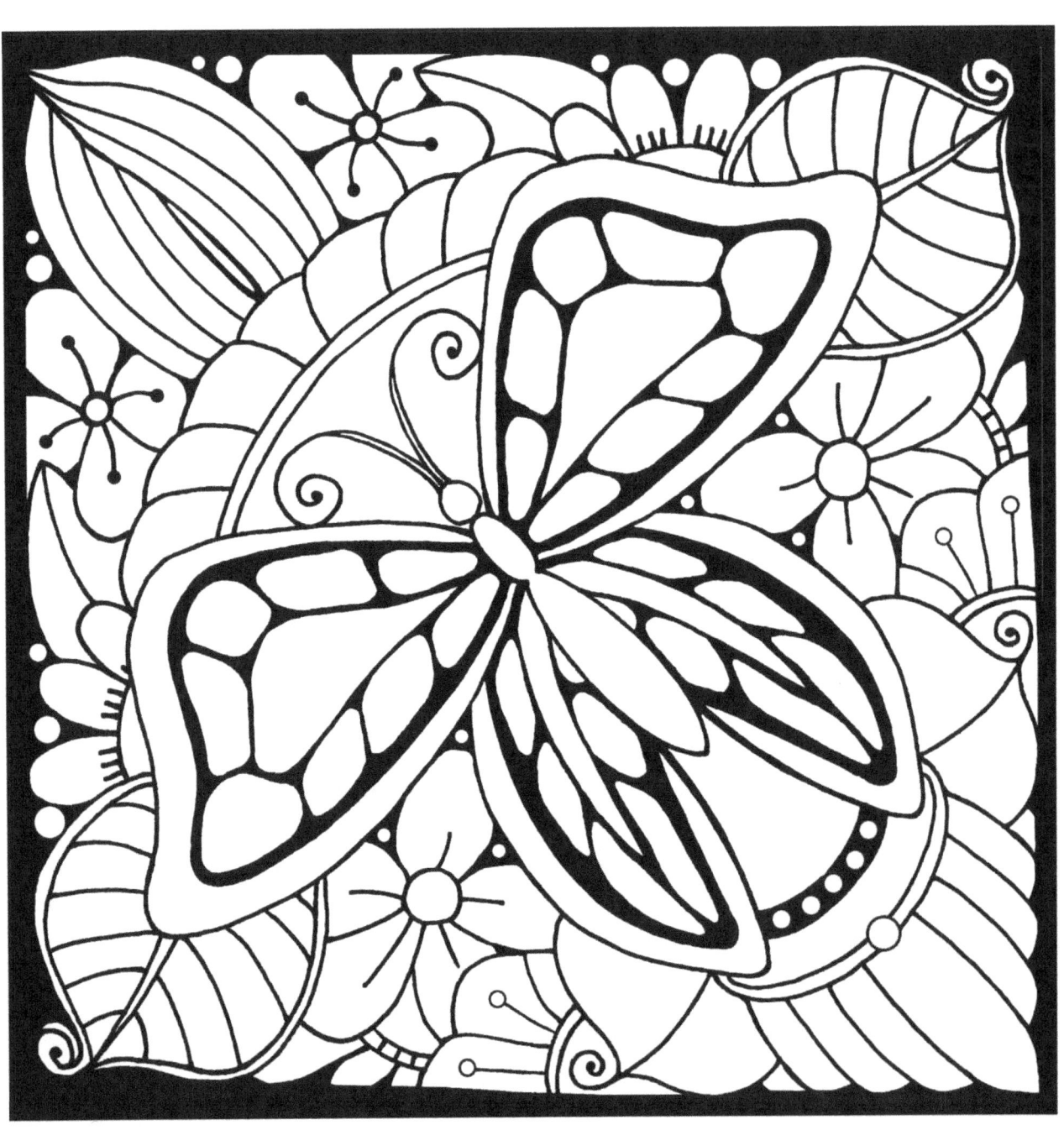

...

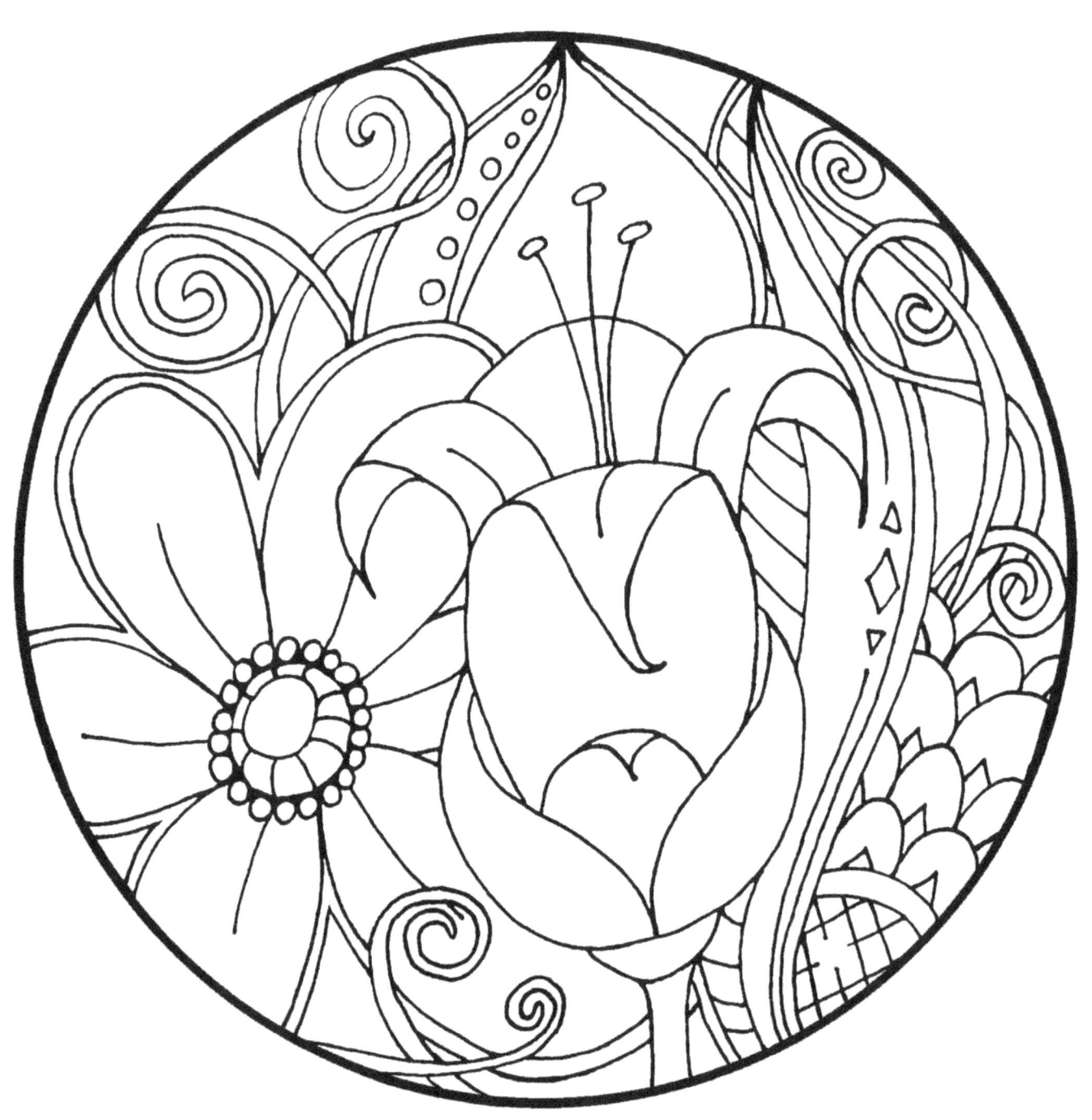

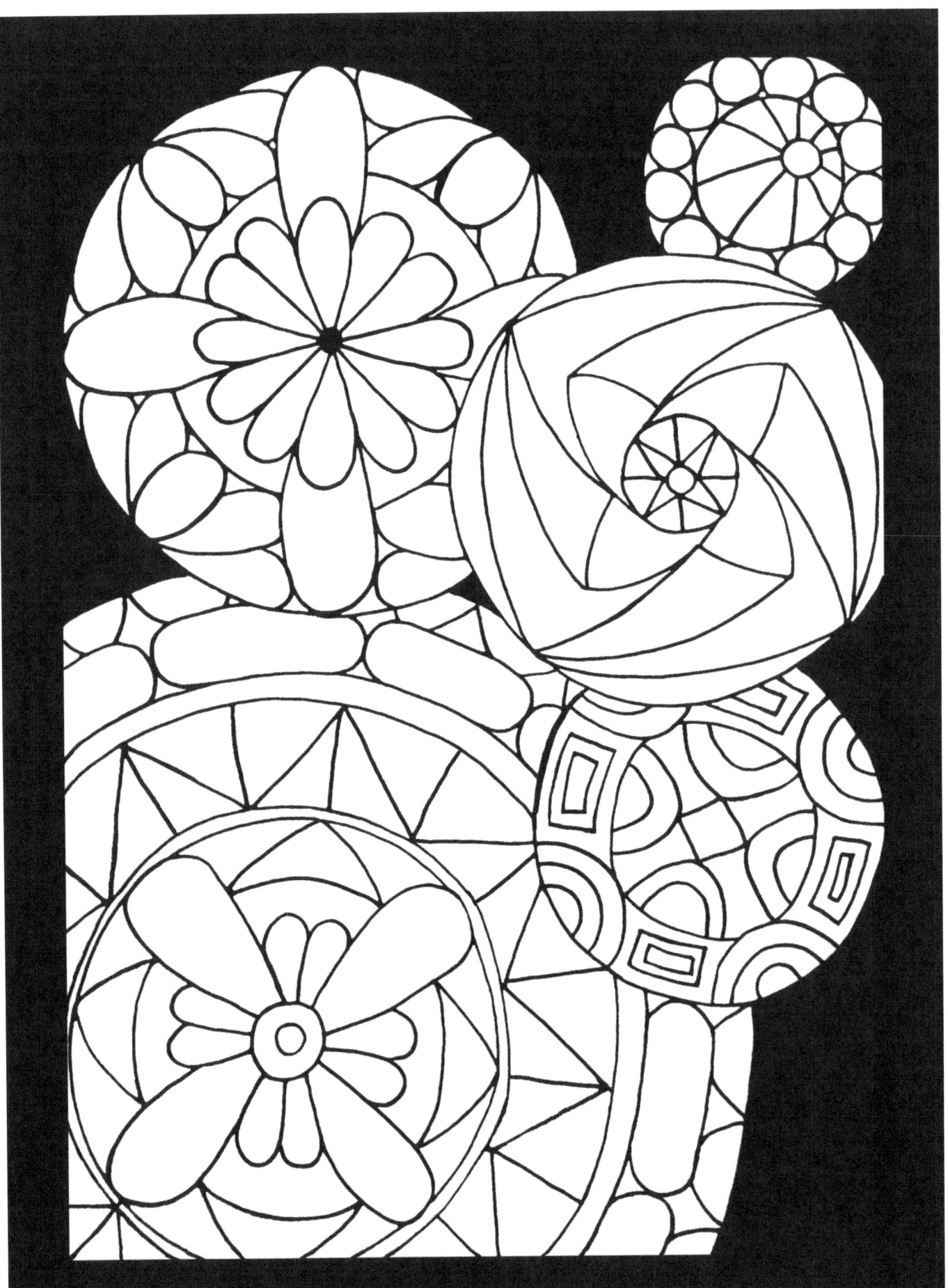

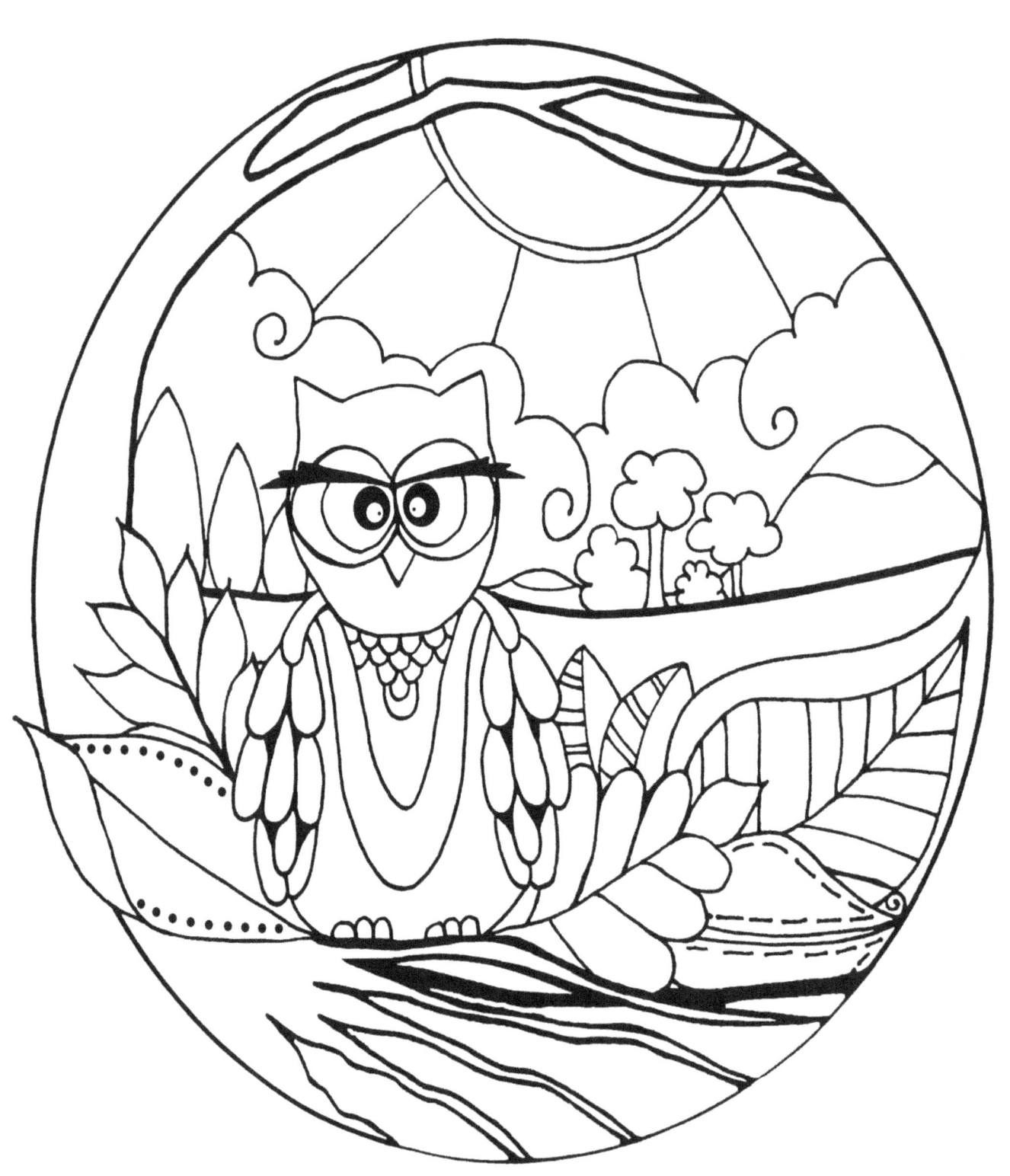

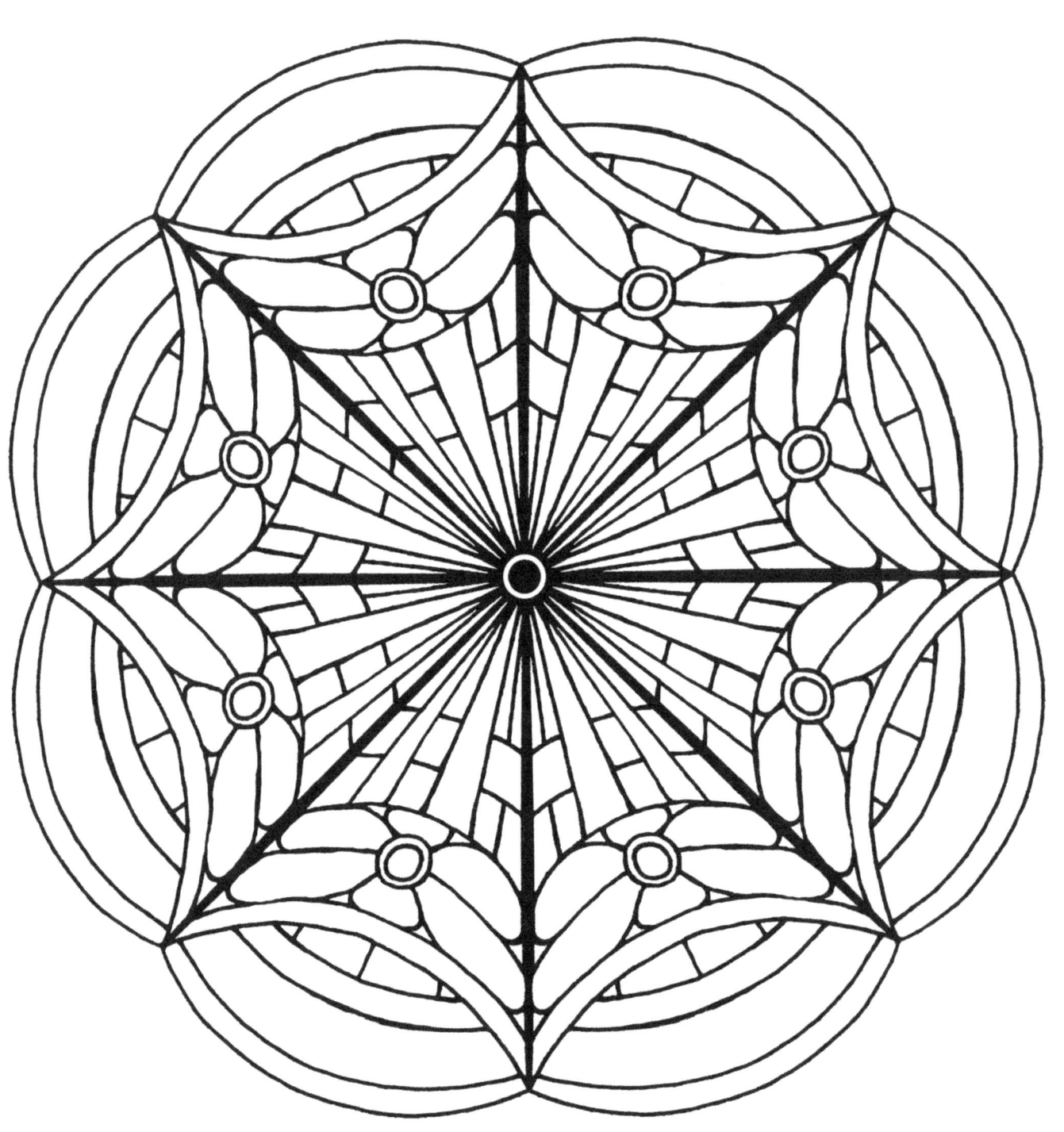

...

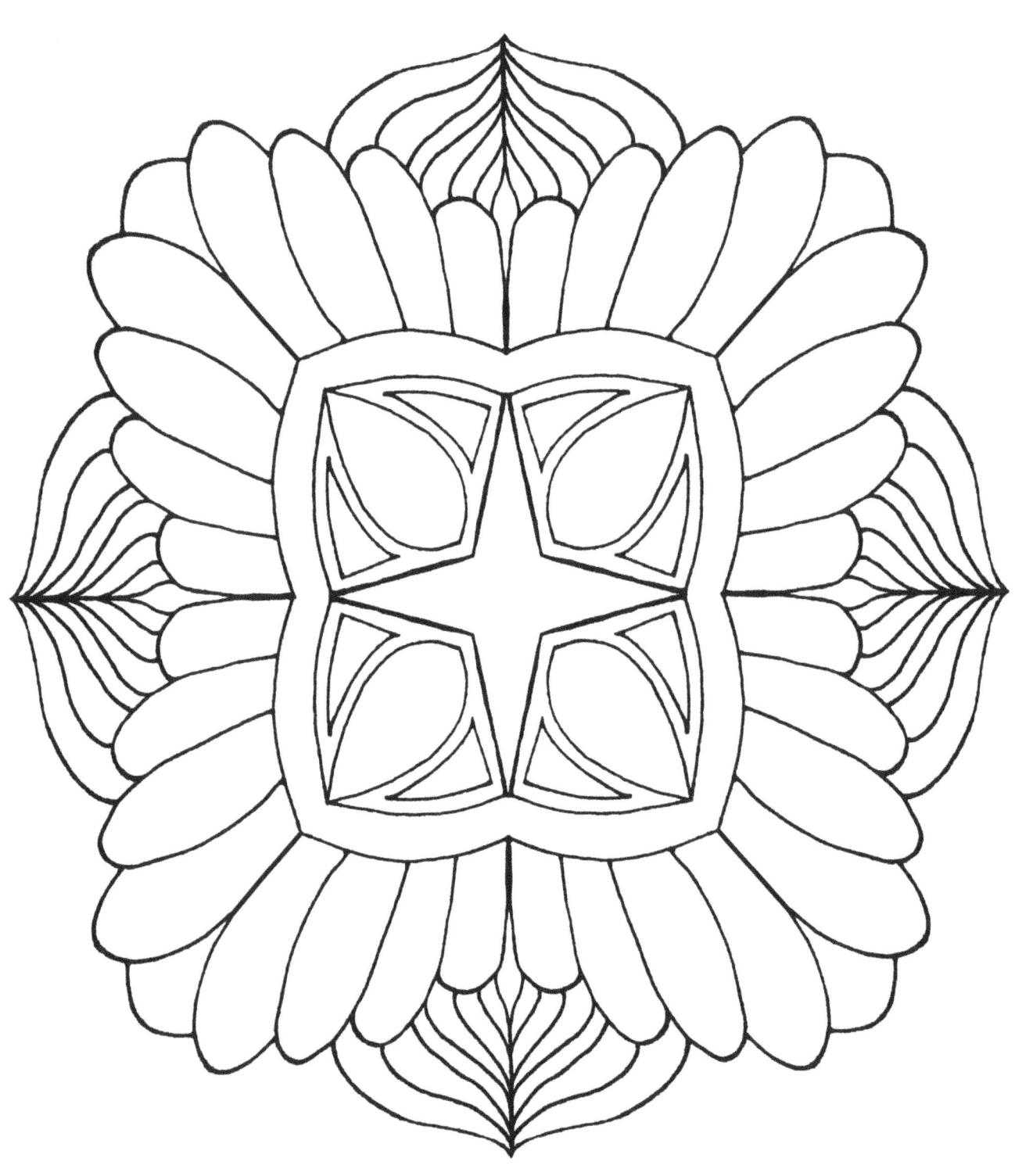

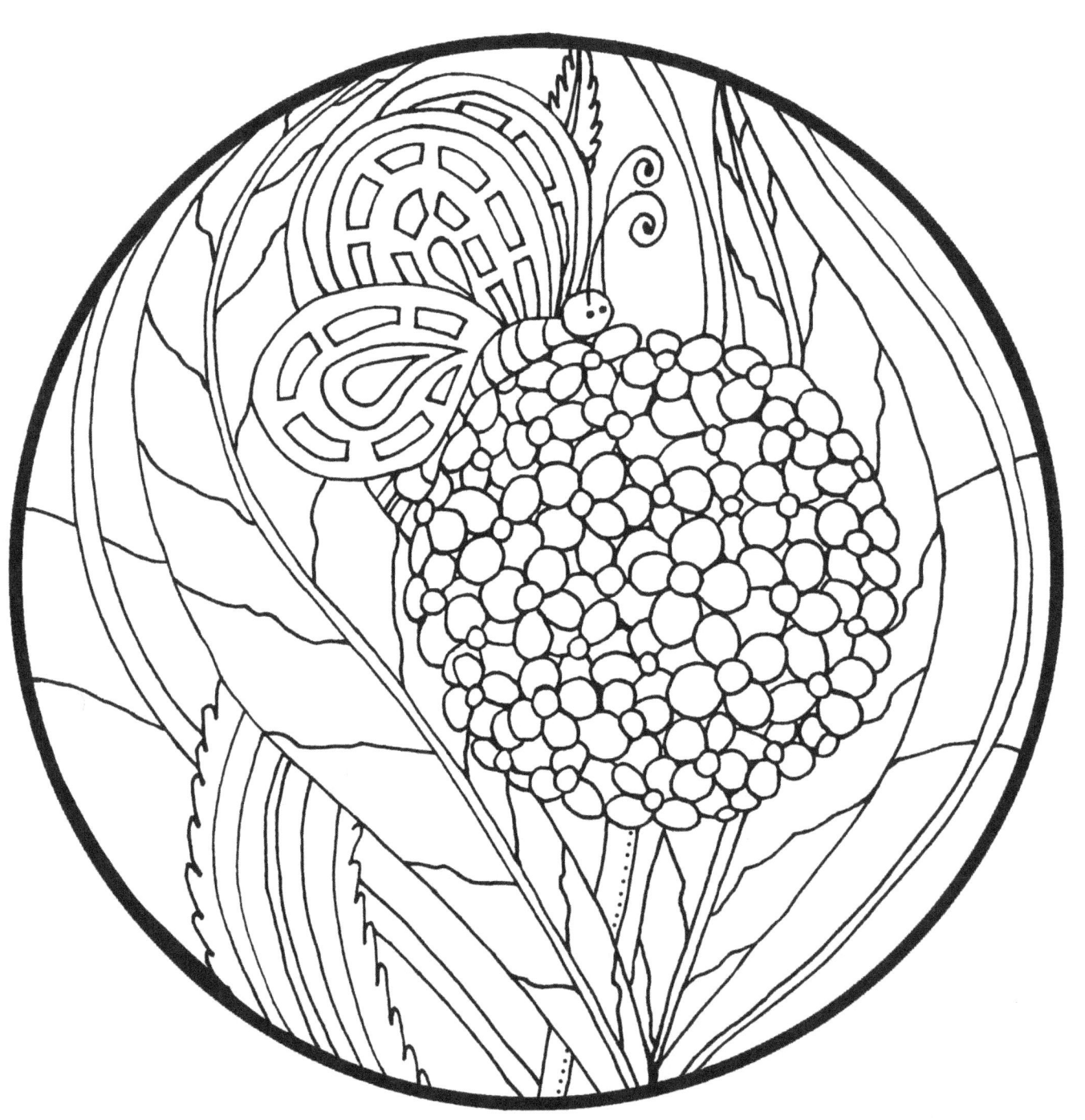

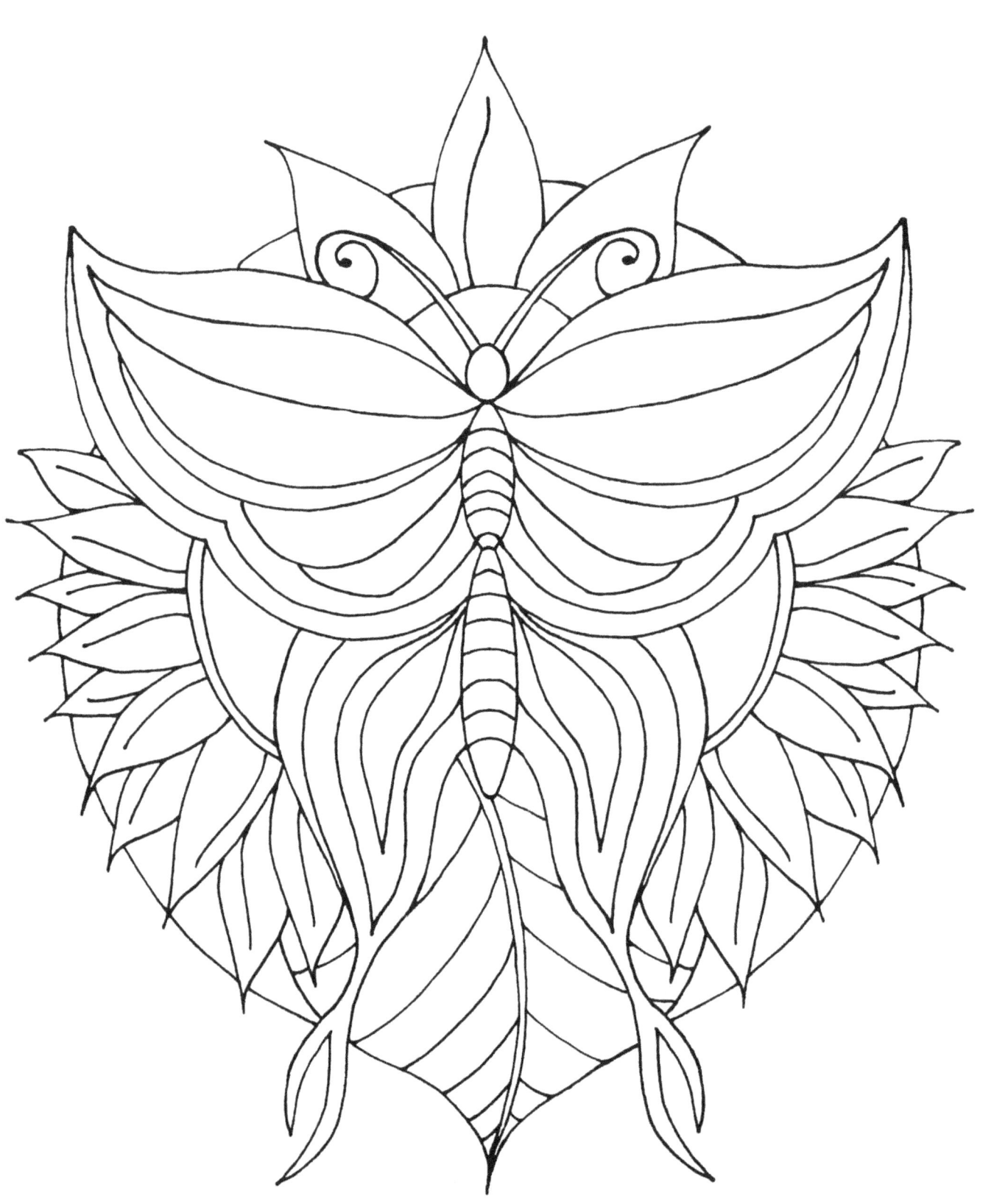

...

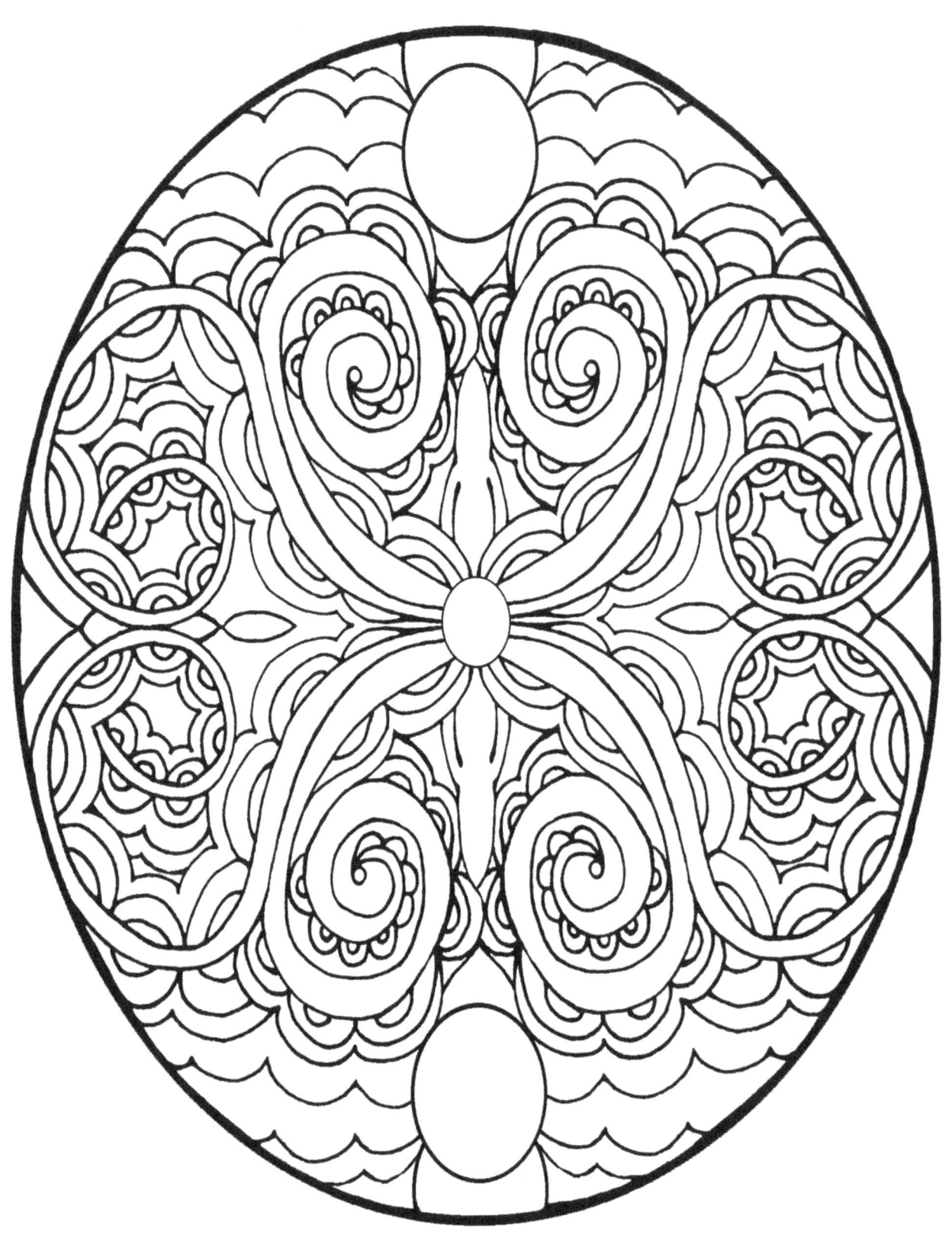

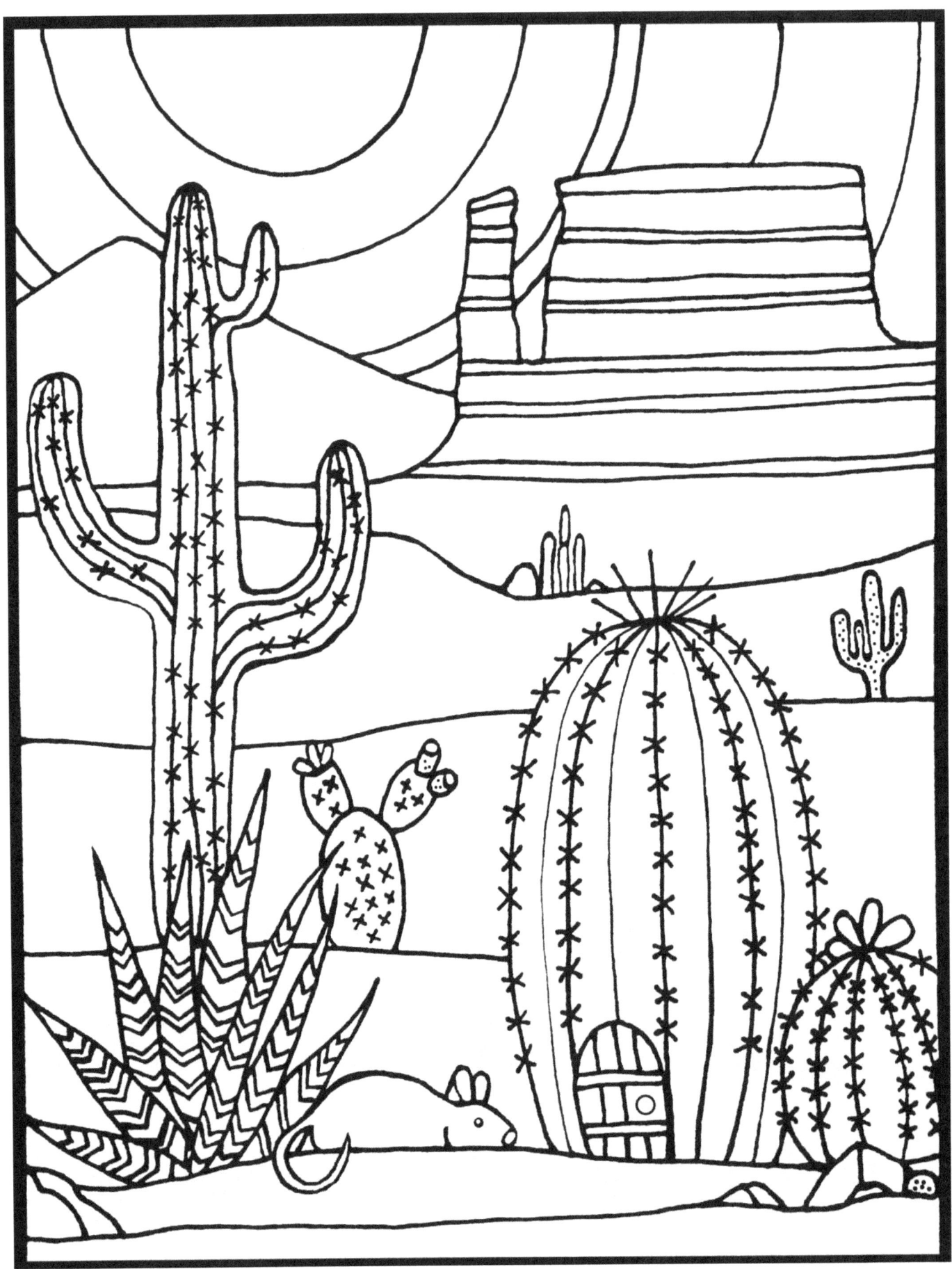

...

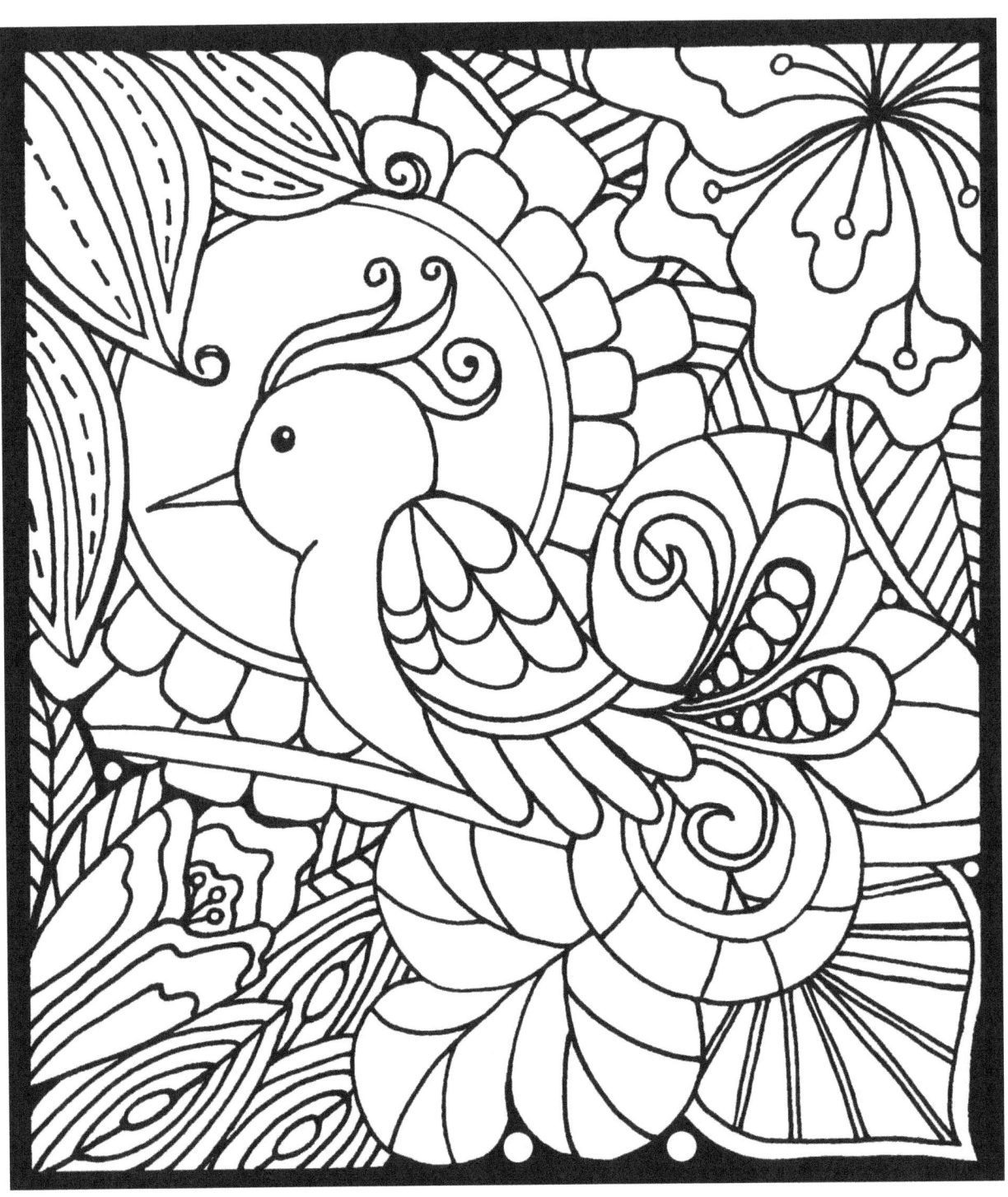

...

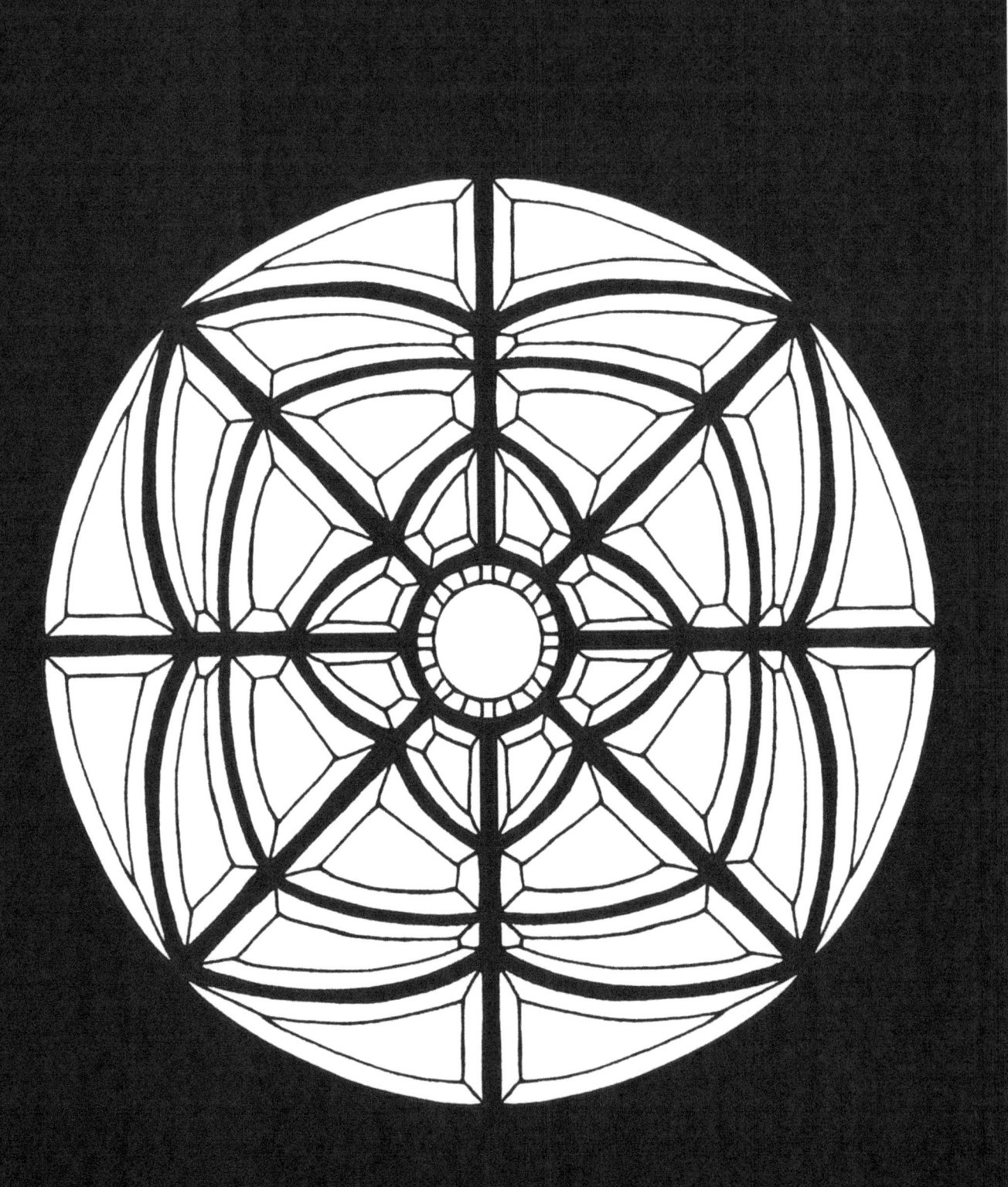

...

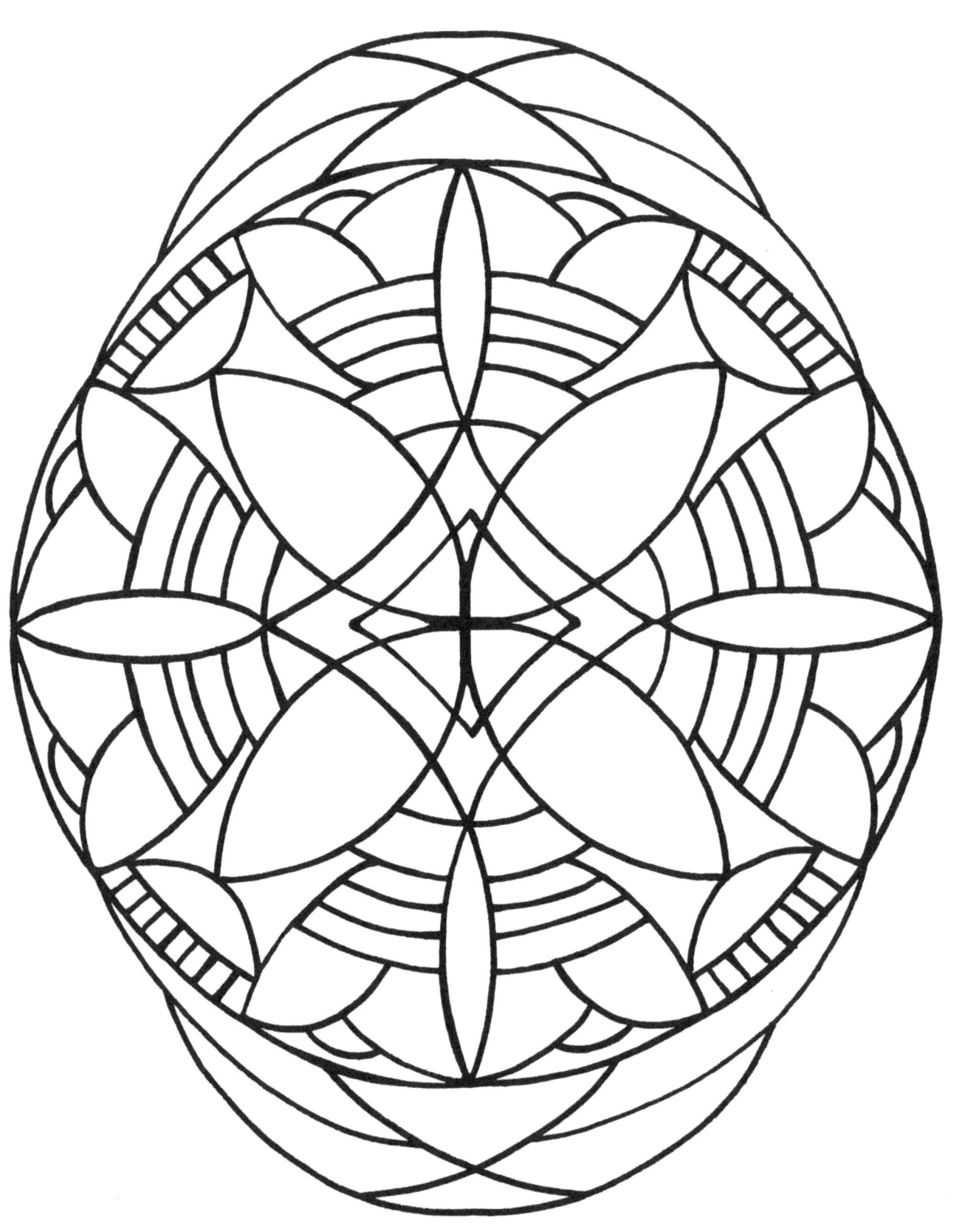

...

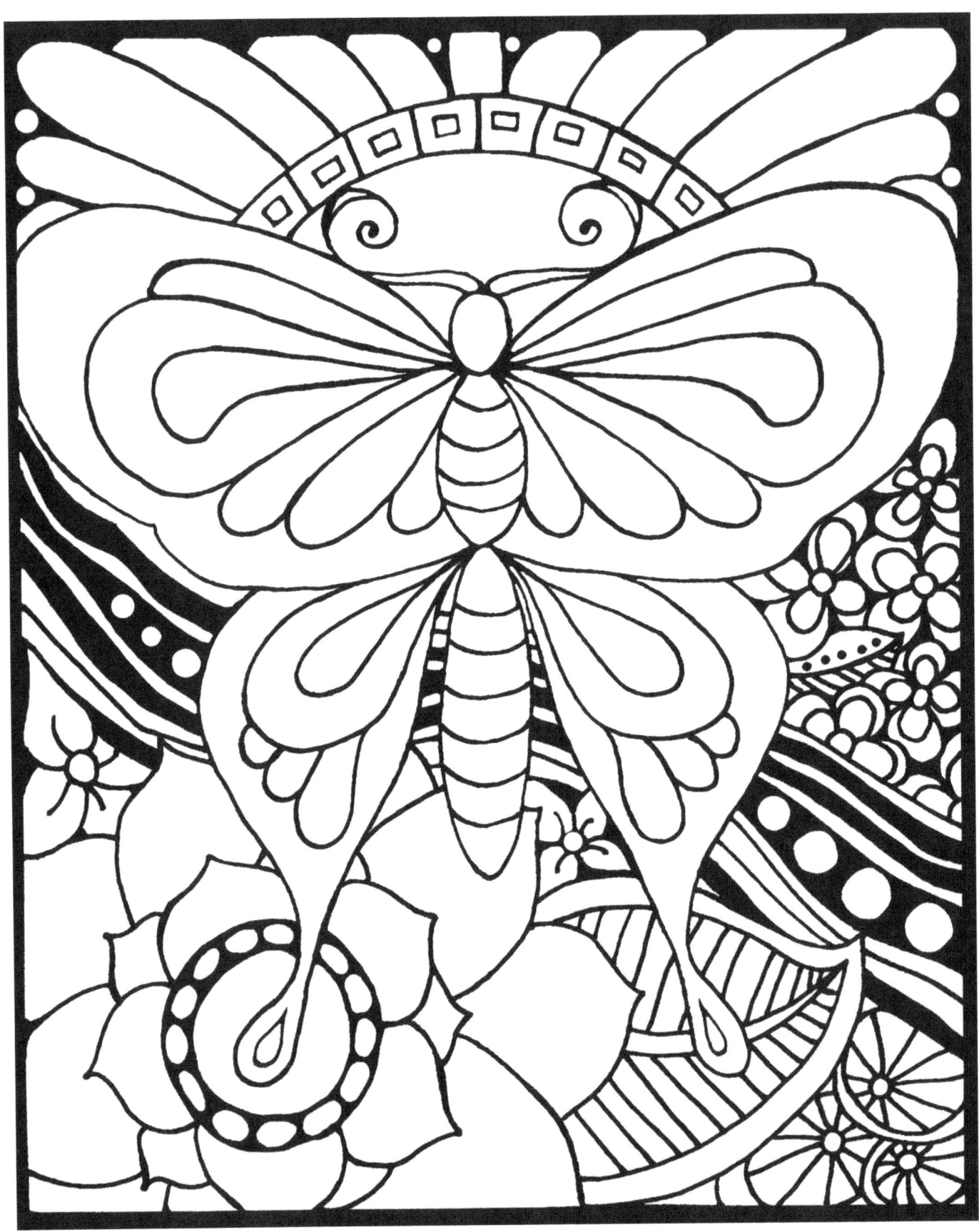

...

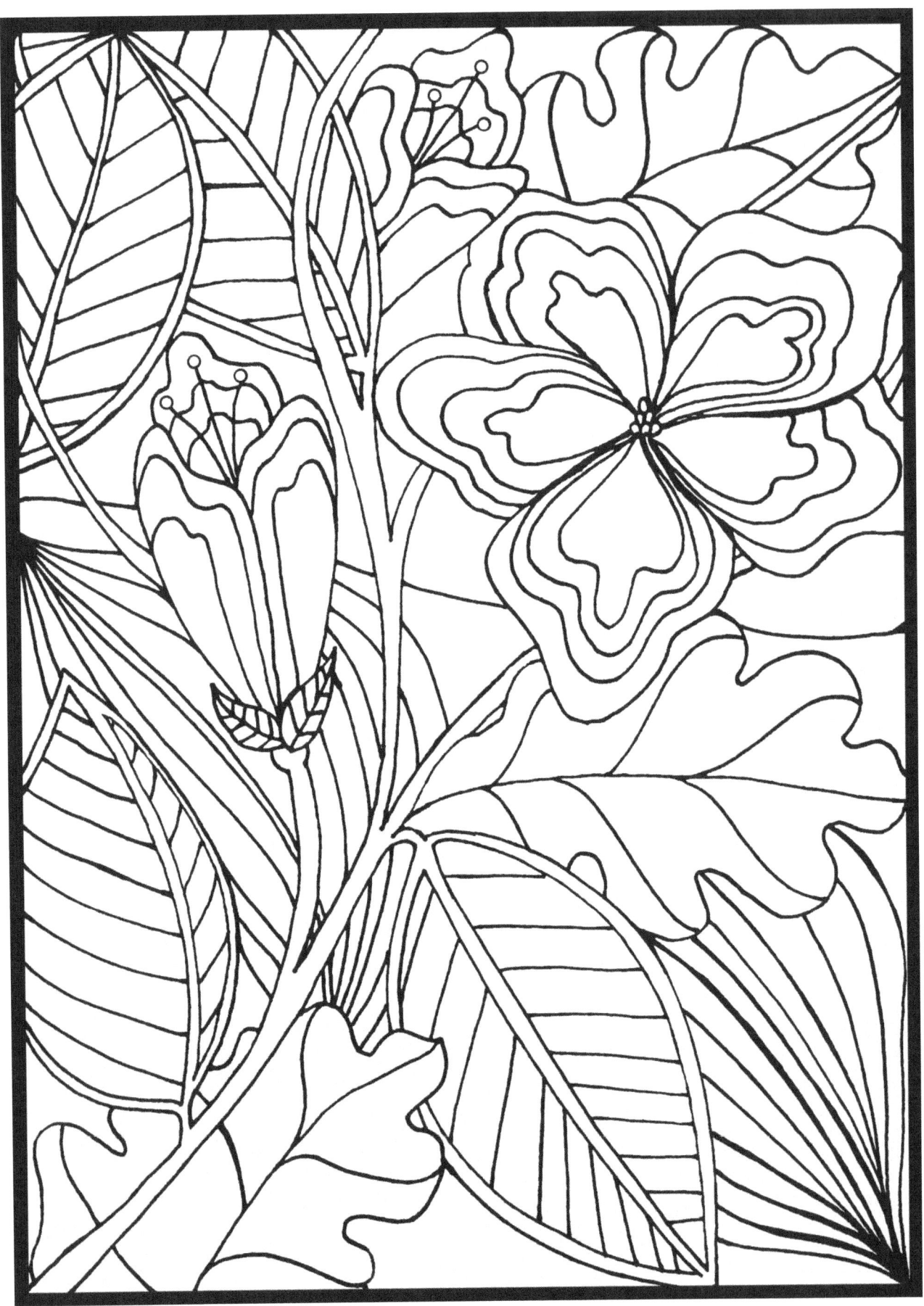

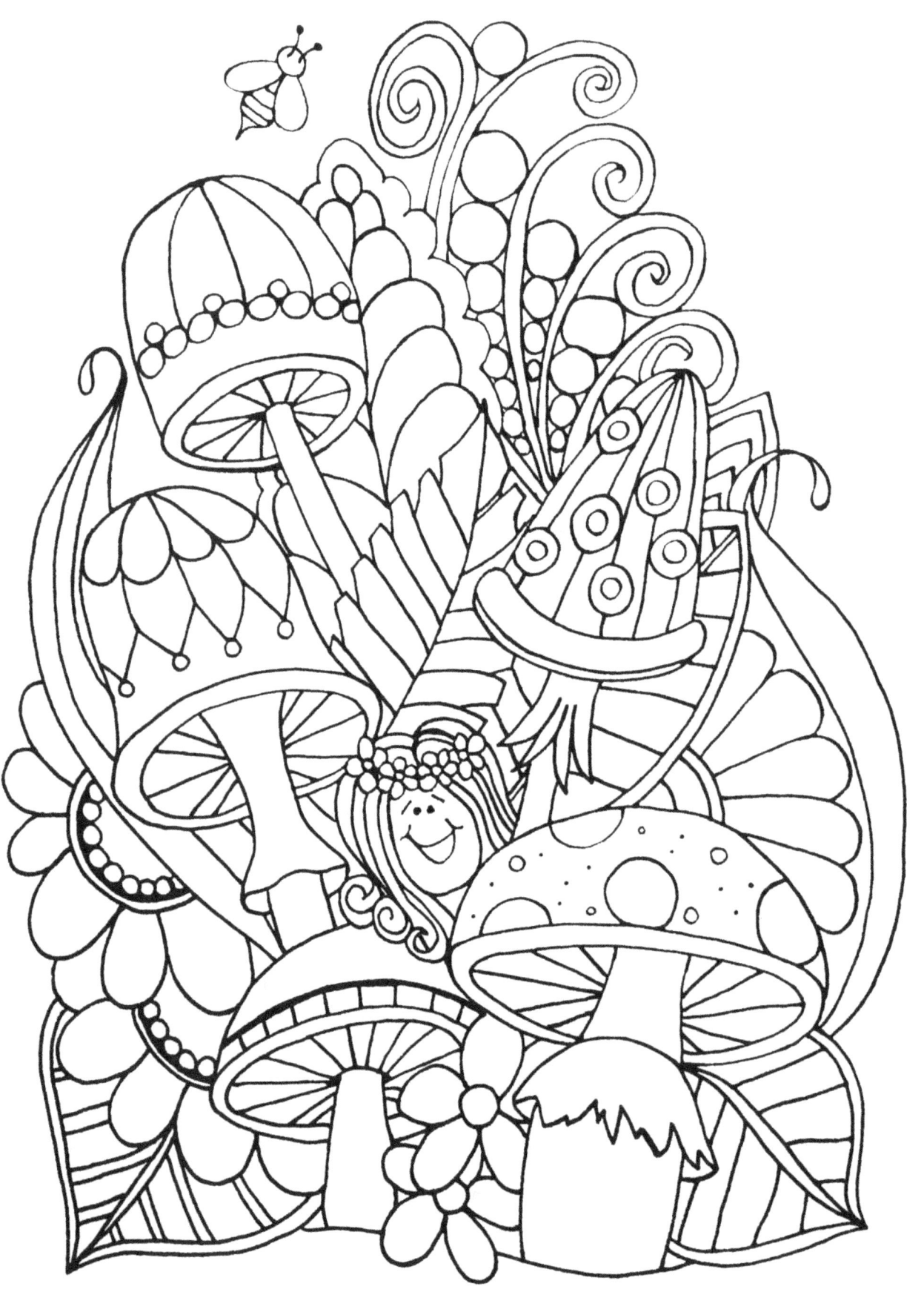

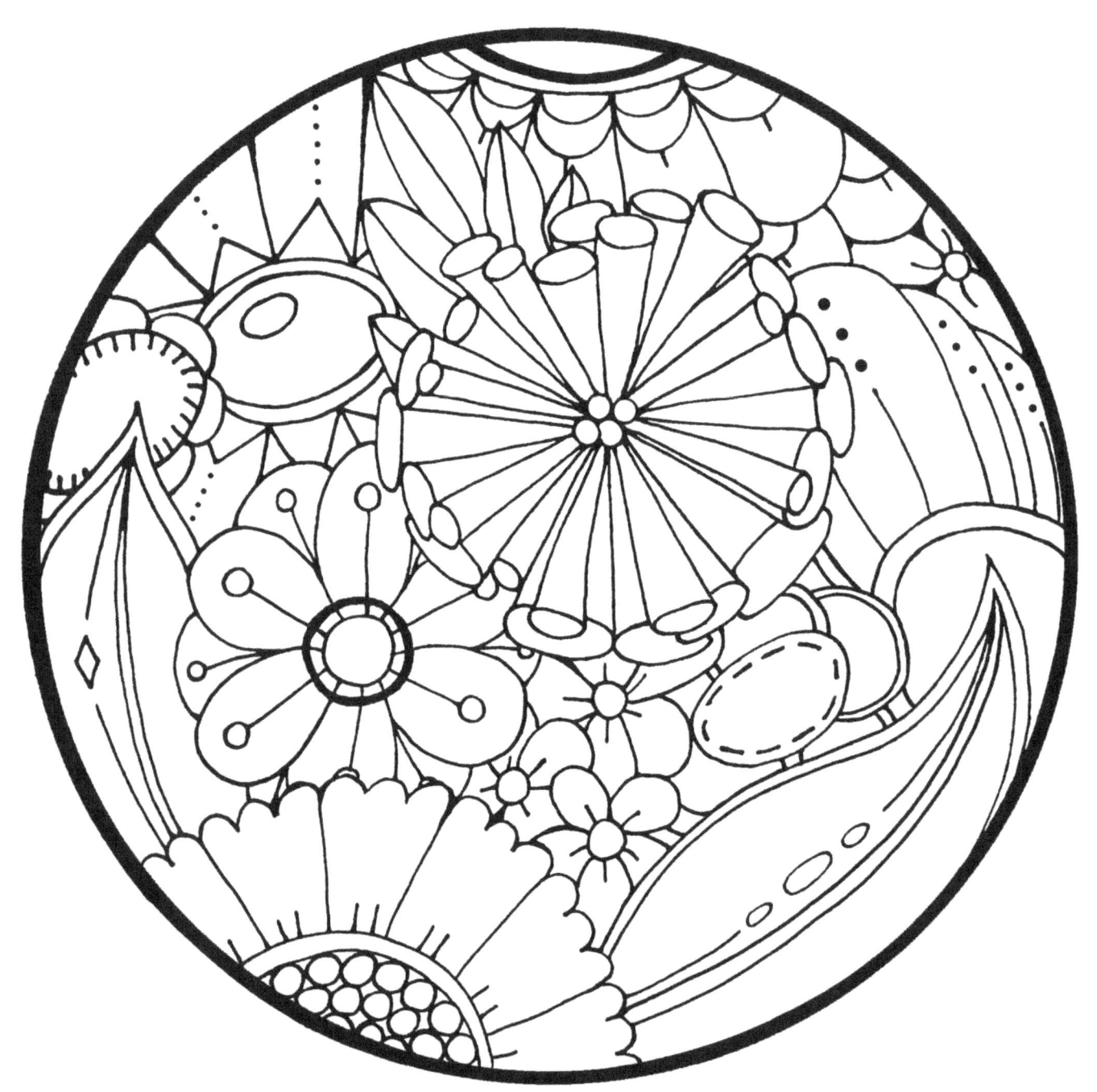

...

...

Color Swatch Paper

...

Color Swatch Paper

...

...

Color Swatch Paper

...

Color Swatch Paper

...

www.ingramcontent.com/pod-product-compliance
Lightning Source LLC
Chambersburg PA
CBHW081019240526
45471CB00017B/3425